WHERE'S WIL?

By:

R. J.

ISBN: 978-1-7363669-5-0
Published By: InspiredByVanessa
www.InspiredByVanessa.com

Where's Wil?

Have you guys seen Wil?

Is he here? Is he there?
I cannot find Wil anywhere!

Where's Wil?

I need Wil; he helps me with everything.

He is there when I need him; he is always around, especially when I am sad and down.

Where's Wil?

Wil helps me count my 123s
and helps me sing my ABCs.

Wil is my superhero. He saves
me from the dark; he is the
light that shines so bright.

Wil catches me every time I fall.
He tells me every time,
"You will overcome it all."

Where's Wil?

Who is Wil, you ask? Wil is my
best friend until the end; he has
been there through thick and thin.

Wil teaches me so many new things, from exercising to trying new foods.

Where's Wil?

Who is Wil? Wil is my friend.

Wil helps me with everything.

Wil says that I can win.

Wil is the best, better than the rest.

Where's Wil?

I found Wil; he's here!

Wil was over there, standing behind me!

I told Wil never to leave me.

About the Authors

Jade R Bryant-Moore was born and raised on the southside of Chicago. She's oldest of five siblings, raised by my grandmother from a young age and instilled I was destined for greatness. Jade excelling elementary with academic honors and graduating top ten in my senior class from Chicago International Charter School Longwood Campus. She knew at that moment she was at the top to have a minor setback in college but finally finished in July 2020 with her Bachelor's in Correctional Support Services with two honor societies under my belt with a GPA of 3.4. She then decided to attack her Masters in Clinical Mental

Health Counseling also being a mother of five beautiful kids excelling in motherhood.

Jade is also a Local School Council Chairwoman at Brennemann Elementary and Outreach Coordinator in Parent Advisory Council. She is a force to be reckon with and making changes by bringing awareness to her community and being a part of so many elite outreach organizations.

Jade started her own outreach group called Mother's of Women Outreach on Facebook, bringing positive and motivational words to women across the world. Jade is a formidable parent that believes in investing in her children because they hold the future.

This book was meant to convey a message of greatness to young girls. I am a powerhouse, a highly active mom, and I am a firm believer in advocating for our children. Being the Local School Council Chairperson for my children's school Brennemann Elementary and also the Outreach Coordinator for Parent Advisory Council, I am a formidable parent that believes in investing in her children because they hold the future.

Feel free to follow me on Facebook at:

www.FamilyXpressions.com
https://www.facebook.com/jadie.wadie.9
https://www.facebook.com/groups/702779853500218

www.ingramcontent.com/pod-product-compliance
Lightning Source LLC
Chambersburg PA
CBHW042006100426
42736CB00038B/131